BUCKWHEAT CAKES
and
CORNMEAL MUSH

(Growing Up In The Thirties)

By: Shirley Ensrud

Shirley Ensrud

i

CONTENTS

In Memory
of my Dad,
Bixler Baker,
who would have been proud

FOREWORD

In this, my first book of poems, I take you into my childhood northwest of Mankato, MN, where I somehow garnered the viewpoint that one can do whatever she thinks she can.

Knowing that my poetry is not overly literary, but with the feeling that it is very accessible, I am publishing it in the hope it will bring you enjoyment and possibly evoke various emotions.

This is an attempt to share my memories of the past with my contemporaries, and to enlighten my grandchildren and their peers.

ANNA'S PITCHER

As Anna wrapped the pitcher in her everyday gray gown
she pondered why her Willis felt this bent for forging west.
Two daughters grown, three tiny mounds at churchyard in the town
must needs remain. She started putting treasures in a chest

already lined with lap robes and the quilts she had produced
with help of elder daughters and her mother. She would miss
them all. The spring fed water and wild fruits that they had juiced
were part of life, entwined with all their family genesis.

Her hands caressed the vessel that she held; pale blue the trees,
the domes of onion shape, the roman columns and the dress
of ladies, gentlemen, the likes she'd never known. Her cheese,
fresh milk must have attention. How'd she let her mind digress?

She must evoke an air of calm, the children, too, were loath
to leave their friends, all that they knew. To leave some toys,
as she, herself, must choose which implements she'd need for both
utility and sentiment. Her heart swelled for her boys,

all four. They'd help their father who would homestead, who would farm.
He'd dicker and their life would be nomadic for some time;
set up a homesite, settle in. He didn't feel alarm
at uprootings. And Anna's place would be to yield her prime.

She couldn't know all this that day in eighteen ninety-eight--
or was there a presentiment? She bade the girls get dressed.
They knew their tasks on normal days but now she must mandate
some final little task for them, and nurse one at her breast.

The children grew to fine adults. They married, all but three.
Young Nellie, tender, teaching school, put off her own frail health
in favor of her students, but her life was not to be
long lived. Her letters and her zest were what she left as wealth.

The kinfolk came to Anna's house to offer comfort, love;
she filled the pitcher, poured the glasses near to overflow.
She filled her day receiving them with thought to comfort of
her guests, the only way of meeting stress she'd ever know.

1

The sons all wed, two daughters stayed till parents took their rest
from mortal toil. The maiden ladies chose the nearest town
for their new home, and Anna's pitcher poured to many a guest.
The sisters sewed for countless folks and gained no small renown.

Their niece is proud to have her Grandma's pitcher on display
with other choice antiques. Her father's childhood trip that crossed
six states by rattling train, his boyhood spent behind a bay
horse, Fleet by name and fleet by disposition are embossed

upon her memory from stories that he told, retold.
The pitcher passed to him, surviving son of Anna, when
his sisters died. His mind would reach back into days of old
in Pennsylvania where they all began. Much simpler then

was lifestyle, Mother Anna mostly at the kitchen stove,
the children taking turns at bringing water from the spring,
the mother canning jelly from the fruits out in the grove,
and Papa pushing him and siblings in the rope-held swing.

His daughter mulls these thoughts each time she sees the pitcher, blue
and white, a regal tie to all her heritage. She leaves
her home each day for work not like her grandmother's. So few
who see the pitcher glimpse the loving pattern that it weaves

together. Her descendants plan continuing its flow
from parent down to child in generations not conceived.
And Anna would be proud to see her pitcher spread its glow
into another century, and happily received.

BIOGRAPHY

Betraying bachelorhood,
Bixler betrothed beloved bride,
baptized booteed babies,
barbered boys,
bolted broken bicycles,
behove befitting behavior,
bounced begging brood by burnished boot,

2

bestowed basic beliefs,
batted baseballs beyond backfielders,
becalmed breathless bairns bedeviled by blizzard,

became biologist, botanist, breeder, buyer,
bookkeeper, bootblack, builder, businessman,

boasted barn bedding barrows, boars, bovines, bulls,
built brooders bounding broilers,
butchered beef,
buckled breechings,
broke broncos, bridled bays,

brandished brace-bit, buzzsaw, broadaxe, bucksaw,
broadcast barley, binned beans,
battled blight, burdocks, burrs, bugs,

buttered breakfast buckwheats,
blessed baked beans, blanc-mange, bacon, berries,

branded biblical blasphemers banal,
berated bullies, boozers. backbiters,
befriended brothers, bumpkins, bourgeois.

Beguiled by baseball bullpens, billiards, bands,

beleaguered by bills,
bargained, bartered belongings,
banished belligerence,
brought belief, bounded back,
behaved blamelessly, befitting bold background.

Biased bipartisan, bantered before balloting.

Baldness bloomed,
bifocals bested blurring,
bowlegs betrayed bent bones.

Buick bypassed buckboards, buggies, bobsleds.
Bixler Baker bequeathed boundless blessings
beyond burial bier;

backbone, beneficence, belief,
brotherhood, buoyancy, birthright,
benediction.

A CHILD, A HORSE AND A MAN

Her mount obliges, plods on to the end
of lane, then turns without a signal from
the child, bare-legged upon his back, who's begged
her father for the privilege to ride
astride this beast, more used to heavy toil.

She, unimpressed by power, brute strength beneath
the broadness of his back, relaxes as
his gait is faster, homeward bound. He bears
her gently, never condescendingly,
between the fields where daily he applies
his brawn to pull the seeder, mower, plow
the length of heavy, black, productive soil.

Forgotten are the days beside his dam
when he ran free of bridle, bit and rein.
His lot is bearing burdens gross or light
determined by an overall clad man;
a man who rubs him down when sweaty, hot,
and spells him often when the sun is high,
provides the oats, the water, hay and straw--
the creature comforts he has earned and more;
who broke him without whip eons ago
and yearly set a child upon his back
(all nine, and now this skinny sprite who knows
she is a circus bareback rider, he
an elephant. She glows, waves to the clown.)

Rox ends the ride, and as she knows he will,
he steps across the sill into the barn.
Her arms about his neck, her head on mane,
she lies until her father lifts her down.

TESTING GERMINATION

He sprinkled kernels of corn
in cloth-lined tins,
folded corners over,
dampened them with water;

placed the samples
in wood range
warming oven
and waited--
which lot would sprout first,
or more hardy shoots?

DeKalb and Pioneer
might scoff,
but his harvest
fed and clothed his family.

NOT A TV TOWER

Broken necks,
miraculously,
never resulted
when brothers
plummeted
from second level
under homemade parachutes.

Silent prayers
and covered eyes
certainly
kept Father from falling
when he climbed the tower
to oil the fan.

Bottom ladder was removed
to deter little feet.

Prairie landscape
was once broken
at most farm places
by their looming shapes.

Now windmills
remain
only in pictures
or disrepair.

RE-TIRING AT AN EARLY AGE

He twists metal lid
from round, cardboard container,
shakes out contents,
replaces lid, rubs
inner tube stretched over knee
with rough metal end.

When dull and smooth enough,
squirts vile-smelling
sticky liquid on.

With aplomb of waiter
lighting crepes suzettes
he sets it afire,
blows out flame,
waves it in the air,

peels backing
from red, rubber, rounded-edged patch,
attaches it to spot prepared;
gives new life
to Model A Ford (or bicycle) tire.

This "thirties" Sunday afternoon rite
fascinates watching kids
who wait for him to pitch a few
for weekly softball game.

THE COBBLER WHO WAS OUR FARMER FATHER

To upright iron arm nailed
to sawed-off piece of tree trunk,
he attached a last.
There were tiny forms for baby shoes,
large for his own and big brothers',
medium for ours.

He resembled a walrus
with his mouth full of tacks
he placed, one by one,
near very edge
of leather he had shaped
and tapped them fast,
felt inside to ease his mind
that none might bruise our toes.

Mending extended
useful life of footwear
handed back to owners
or passed to younger siblings.
With new heels or soles
we skipped along,
for we knew farm kids
who walked on folded newspapers
stuffed inside their shoes.

CHOCOLATE-COVERED CHERRIES

One said her Grandpa loved them,
another that her husband's father did.
Jill said she hadn't had them for years
and Mary that they were a Christmas memory.

Four boxes of sweets;
a token, only to co-workers,
each emotional
when thanking me.

7

The gesture sprang from my own reaction
when I saw them in the store.
As a child I gave them to my Dad
and he popped the first one into my mouth.

OUR PROTECTOR RETURNS

Lightning splits
dark, noisy sky.
Leaves blow from trees,
sheets whip on lines.
Mother leads us to cellar
where we huddle together.

I pray for Dad to come
from the field,
peek between fingers
that block out shadowy corners.

We hear cultivator clatter,
horses' hooves enter the barn.
Dad runs through rain
to where we are, grins,
shakes water all over us;
makes us know it will be all right.

OVER-TIPPED

The men were strangers;
they mentioned a town.
"My Dad lived there once," I said.
They asked me his name
and one of them cried,
"He sold me his bay when he wed."

They then reminisced
while eating their meal.
I served them their salad and main course.
he left me a tip,
a ten dollar bill,
"Because that was such a darn good horse."

WHERE'D THE FUNNIES GO?

What ever happened
to the Katzenjammer Kids?
Where are Maggie and Jiggs?
We lay prone on Sunday afternoons
passing the colored section
forth and back
and father laughed out loud.

Little clouds with pointed bottoms
are full of satire now--
political and feminist;
but where is Barney Google--
silly enough to make kids giggle
and their dad laugh out loud?

PERSISTENT MEMORY

I nearly nightly have the flash-back
days before Christmas
as I close my office door at five p.m.

Dad is picking me up at S & L
where I work as salesgirl
and it is dark.
It is cold, streets
are festooned,
lights are everywhere,
and I wear a scarf,

gift from first boyfriend.

The fact of early darkness
is base of the memory
but also, there is always
the cold, the lights, the scarf
and my Father.

COUNTRY HAIRCUTS

One by one we climbed up on the stool,
sat dishtowel-draped like sofas in deserted houses
as he snipped and shaped, blew on our necks.

His specialties were dutch-boy cuts for girls,
spiked for boys, though we called it
something else then.

Work-rough hands, deft with scissors and comb,
performed one more art the prairie farmer
was called upon to do.

The big girl did not want it so short
her ears would show;
the little boy wanted a hole on top
like Dad's.

Once, when he was old,
I cut my father's hair.

BUTCHERING DAY

We little ones were not allowed
to watch the slaughter.
Big brothers helped.
Mother kept us in the kitchen
where she boiled water,

sisters washed Mason jars.
We peeked out later,
saw the carcass strung up on the very limb
where our swing hung in summer.

It was mostly done in winter--
perhaps since chores were lighter
or that the meat not spoil.
I remember a half or quarter
on the table.
Dad with sharpened knife and cleaver
cut pieces he would later
grind to hamburger or sausage,
or Mom would press into jars,
season, process in the oven.

Pennsylvania Dutch heritage
had them utilizing every part.
Organs were cooked.
I never ate them.
Juices stirred into a concoction
called ponhaws Mom cut into slices,
fried on the griddle, and we relished
covered with syrup.

I recall scent of pork fat cooking
and taste cracklings
snitched after lard was rendered.
Hind quarters went to locker in town,
became steaks and roasts, were frozen.

Dad's exhaustion was not only physical.
Sacrificing an animal he had raised
for his family table
was an emotional act.

SHARED CHORES

Weekdays, our parlor heater rattled
as Dad shook ashes down--
shook longer than necessary,
we believed,
noise not allowing us
to return to sleep
after his call.

He laid in corncobs and coal,
set fire blazing.

Feet were quickly stockinged and shod
to escape tundra floor.
Big boys pulled on
flannel shirts and overalls,
little kids dashed downstairs
in pajamas
to lay clothes on that heater,
pull them warm onto their bodies.

On Sundays, Mother made the fire
and we all slept later,
though not much.

As I set our thermostat
I wonder
how that division of duties
ever evolved.

WARM OR PROUD?

I see leg warmers
snuggly, baggy, rumpled
adorning
tall girls' limbs
and sagging
to little girls' ankles.

I remember
carefully tucking and patting
long underwear as smoothly
as small fingers could,
under white stockings

only to draw them above my knees
as soon as Mother
left my sight.

EARLY MORNING WALK

Deftly
I pace my stride
to avoid turned ankles
on railroad ties,

remember childhood years
of eluding cracks in sidewalks,
that I might not break
my mother's back.

CELERY AND CRANBERRIES

November feast
was homegrown, mostly,
though Mother indulged
our appetites
with store-bought celery
and cranberries.
I still layer those crimson
berries (as she did)
with whipped cream
and crushed graham crackers
in my best glass bowl.
The brown, the white, the red
produce fireworks

in our mouths!

I chop and saute celery
for stuffing,
remember
how we rinsed stalks
in cold water, served them
crisp, fragrant, uncut,
with leaves intact, upright
in a water glass.

Thanksgiving annually conjures
that image of the celery sentinel.

PROGRESSION OF WASH DAYS

While snow ridges at hedges
I fold warm-from-the-dryer linens
into neat little piles.

I see you (on that cold screened porch)
pour steaming water from pail
brought from boiler in kitchen
into Maytag, pump
gas motor crank with your foot.

Air is blue with its sputtering,
second rinse blue
from liquid you pour into it,
your fingers blue from pinning
underwear and sheets onto lines;
and again from bringing them in
frozen, like plywood.

I hope that machine
was enough improvement
over your mother's washboard and wringer
that you, too, felt blessed.

GRIDDLE CAKES

Mother stirs buckwheat flour
into sour-smelling
bubbly batter set last night,
stuffs corncobs into range
until stove top glows hot,
spreads lard on griddle
with rag tied to fork.

Six man-sized cakes
cover griddle at a time
and they never overlap
when she turns them!
She stacks them on a plate
until choremen come in.

I see overalls all around the table,
hear, "Please pass the syrup,"
the kind made by boiling
brown sugar and water.

Dad finished his chores eight years ago.
Mother thanks nurses
for boiled breakfast eggs.
She says, "We have pancakes
for supper sometimes.
They're not as good as mine."

MOTHER'S HOMEMADE FUDGE

Amongst the caramels and cherry drops,
the chocolate covered coconuts and cremes
in little, shiny fluted paper cups
are candies that some fantasize in dreams.

The Easter gumdrops always make a hit
and children pick the colors they like best.
How often they will search to find a black;

then gladly share with others all the rest.

In February, candy hearts inform
of love, desire and sweetness on their shapes.
Then in the fall we purchase candy corn
as witches ring our doorbells, wearing capes.

At Christmas time the candy canes come out;
divinity and peanut brittle shine,
and parents tell their little ones of love
with gifts galore beneath a tinseled pine.

But I remember tasting parents' love
by searching through a light brown paper sack;
to push aside the nuts and store-bought sweets
for Mother's fudge. Just thinking takes me back.

WHO ARE THEY?

From childhood I heard of them...
ephemeral beings
passing through our existence.
Often,
sometimes daily,
they ruled our lives.

> They don't wear those.
> They don't talk like that.
> What if they see?
> What if they hear?
> They will know.
> They will laugh.
> What will they think?
> What will they say?

And to this day
I do not know who "they" are.

AND NO MOUSSE, EITHER

Overheard:
"You say you have
two teen-aged girls--
and how many bathrooms
do you have?
Just one? Impossible!"

My mother raised nine children
on the prairie
during the depression.
And how many baths had she?
None!

LEONA AND ANNETTE

Turn of the century born,
they became friends in late '20s
when our family moved to the field
across from theirs.
Sturdy farmers' wives
in apron-covered cotton dresses,
they planted zinnias and nasturtiums,
beans, beets, carrots and cucumbers,
then harvested and preserved.

They sent sons to World War II,
wore Mothers' pins--
hers with one star, Mother's with three--
wrote V-Mail letters, anxiously waited
for replies from places they had never known,
pinched dimes from grocery money
for little kids to buy victory stamps,
carefully used coffee and sugar rations.

Each helped the other cook for threshers.
With nine children to feed,
meat, potatoes and chocolate cake were Mom's forte.

She, mother of four, perhaps with more time
or possibly just Swedish instinct,
turned out rosettes and sandbakkels.
Mother played piano for family enjoyment
and for the neighborhood Ladies' Aid,
though she was not Lutheran.

During "The Depression"
they made homes with more love than money,
packed sandwiches and apples, spring and fall,
alternated with other mothers
taking hot meals to one-room school in winter.

After finalizing preparations for Mom's funeral,
we traveled back to the home town for Annette's,
both having died at 92, three days apart.

COUNTRY PHONE LINE

Sixty years later,
I remember our phone number--2-1;
Some lines had longs and shorts
but ours merely two tones, then one.

Johnsons', across the field west, 4-2.
Mom cranked the wall phone three,
then five times to call Annette
across the road
to set times and dates,
ask about sick children,
or just to gossip.

All were guilty of "rubbering"
when others' numbers rang,
for we heard neighbors' rings
on rural lines.

In the art of "rubbering"
one picked up the receiver carefully,

not making a sound so conversers heard.
If we made noise in the room,
Mom would click her fingers
and we knew it meant, "Be quiet."

But we giggled.

SAUERKRAUT SAGA

Razor sharp cutting edge,
set into center of plank
with wooden box on track attached,
rests on chairs six feet apart.

Kids sit on plank's ends,
keep it steady
that Dad might not lose fingertips
pressing heads of cabbage
against the blade.

For half a day
Mom removes outer leaves,
inspects crisp heads,
hands them to Dad.

Slivers of green
collect in thirty gallon
Red Wing crock below,
mound loosely,
are sprinkled with salt,
pressed down with a plate
held in place by a rock.

For a month, cabbage ferments
in open crock, lends
scent to the cellar;
then is canned and processed.
Throughout winter, quarts

of cold sauerkraut are devoured
at meals weekly
at table set for eleven.

RICH DESSERT

I hand spoons
and electric freezer's dasher
to grandchildren.

At once I am eight years old
sitting on old jackets
thrown across
a wooden bucket
and Dad
is turning the crank.

Big brothers have turned
until it is too hard.
Small brother is placed on my lap;
combined weight
keeps freezer
from twisting in the sink.

Mother opens jar
of home-canned meat,
stirs beans that simmered
all day yesterday.
Sisters set table.

We will soon
have Sunday dinner
with homemade ice cream,
and I won't know we are poor
until much later.

OVEN DOOR

They are seldom left open
any more.
Ours was, often.

After walk home from school
we defrosted feet and hands,
dried mittens there.
Dad warmed "runt" baby pigs
in boxes on the door
to assure survival.

When washtub was filled
with warm water,
we opened the oven
to take the chill
from bathtime.

Best of all
was when Mom opened it
and six loaves of bread,
crusty and hot,
sent their scent
throughout the house.

RADIO, SIXTY YEARS AGO

I hurried home from school
to hear Jack Armstrong's
adventures.
Teen sisters tuned in popular songs
and love stories at Grand Central Station.
Mother followed Stella Dallas and Ma Perkins'
daily joys and frustrations.

Dad, who laughed out loud
at the antics of Amos and Andy,
hoped he should live long enough

to see if they really would
invent a box where you might
actually see, as well as hear,
the entertainers.

BEFORE DAWN ON THE FARM

The boys, warm coated, between them bore
the basket, heavy with cobs
while I, well mufflered, my pails in hand
trudged barnward, doing our jobs.

I held containers below the spouts
where thick, rich cream and milk flowed.
I loved the granary, the red barn where
the kittens purred and cows lowed.

Our daily tasks were stoically done,
each child's assignment his due.
With Dad choremaster, no one might shirk;
and shoddy efforts were few.

The teen-aged brothers helped milk the cows
and whistled, not much in tune.
They knew that Mother was mixing cakes
and they'd be eating them soon.

My sisters, packing noon lunches, glanced
toward the slamming back door
where Dad and choremen brought with them cold
and stamped their feet on the floor.

We then assembled and bowed our heads;
anticipation was great.
Though daily buckwheats were breakfast fare,
we gladly suffered our fate.

GRADE A, PASTEURIZED, HOMOGENIZED, VITAMIN D MILK

How impersonal are milk cartons,
no warmth of a barn
nor scent of animals and hay;
no friendly creatures
that go directly to stalls
and step about, switching tails
when city cousins attempt to milk them.

Few teen-aged boys today
have balanced on one-legged stools,
pail between knees,
nor known satisfaction
of twang, twanging milk into a pail.

Warm from cows, the milk
was poured through a strainer
into separator bowl,
trickled through maze of discs and apparatus.
As boys in overalls turned the crank
milk flowed from one spout,
cream from another.

While respecting Pasteur
and sterile dairy products,
I hark back to carefree times
when kittens licked foamy milk from whiskers
and brothers whistled innocently
while squirting
each other on backs of necks
as they milked the cows.

FAMILY HARVEST, 1935

Farmer draws blue cotton sleeve
across forehead,
peers over horses' backs,
cuts orderly swaths

'round and 'round
perimeter of undulating grain.

Reaper reel creaks,
sickle whispers,
canvas flaps.
There is clicking sound
like ticking of seven-day clocks
as wheat is tied into sheaves.
Flies buzz, horses switch tails.
Clouds float beneath sun,
give brief respite.

Boys in bib overalls
stack gathered bundles
into shocks,
turn prairie into
village of tepees.

Small girl earns praise
for trudging across stubble
with Mother's oatmeal cookies
and tin pail
full of cold water.

BAREFOOT IN SPRING

We did it every year--
sneaked out onto greening grass
while snow still lingered
under bushes.
Bare feet tolerated
the abuse awhile;
we were grateful
when Mother ordered us inside.

Allowed soon after,
tenderfooted, we stayed on grass
at first, graduated

to gravel road tentatively.

By midsummer, our soles
leathery, we bemoaned
Sunday shoes.

Rain showers beckoned us
to undress except for underwear,
to dance in the yard.
Six miles from town,
we had no swim suits,
no swimming pool,
no near neighbors.

Best was going after cows
in the marshy pasture,
mud and green grass
oozing between our toes.

It is sixty years
since I have done it.
I must shed my shoes
and walk around the house
next time it rains.

GIFTS OF THE DEPRESSION

I often bring to mind the pleasant times
and yes, the times of stress and struggle too;
the days we went to matinees for dimes,
the hours we spent in planning things to do,
the nine our parents fed and schooled and clothed,
the buckwheat cakes we loved for breakfast fare,
the cornmeal mush we often ate, and loathed,
the hand-me-downs we were obliged to wear.

Our father, harsh when he was disobeyed,
would waken us at dawn to go to see
the elephants and tigers in parade

from railroad to the circus site for free.

"No gum in Church," Mom stated as a rule
while handing pennies out for Sunday School.

ANGRY ACCUSATION

Oh, thief that robbed us of our heritage,
what need had you of books we knew in youth--
the vet's guide we perused in hermitage
that pictured cow's gestation? We learned truth
of sex and embryos, though slightly versed.
You took Horatio Alger, Jr., too
and Billy Sunday's sermons interspersed
with pictures, and the Bible that we knew.

The desk that held them all, with glassed-in door
and cubbyholes that held those grown-up things
was one small corner, though it was the core
of home where poor folk dwelled, thought they were kings.

Your flames, at least, did not take human soul;
your smoke, long settled, left us less than whole.

I REMEMBER SATURDAY AT THE MOVIES

Roy charges down Main Street,
trusty stallion
kicking up billows of snow.
Bad guys lurk behind post office.
Trigger rises to hind legs
as master reins him in.

Black-hatted men turn horses
down Second, past supermarket
with our hero in pursuit,
swerve at Episcopal Church,

gallop to Thirteenth,
give mounts their heads.

Roy cuts them off at Rice Street,
exaltation evident in his posture.
Posse charges on the scene
so man and horse turn east out of town,
white hat in the air
as Rossini's "William Tell Overture"
breaks into final measure
on car radio.

THANKSGIVING REMEMBERED

Ice clinks in water glasses
as waitress approaches,
announces, "My name is Amy."
Fan blades whirr above, stir the air.
We order entrees, each different,
choose hors d'oeuvres,
vegetables from salad bar,
finish with slivers of cheesecake.

I see past little square tables,
fluttering candles,
into wood-range dominated kitchen.
Silverware clinks as sisters
set table, pulled full length.
I hear aunts murmuring, fire crackling,
potatoes bubbling, soon to be mashed
with chunks of butter stirred in.
Sweet smell of yams covered with marshmallows
mingles with those of roasting turkey
and Mother's home-canned pickles.

Outside, old plow horse is reluctantly
pulling uncle's Model A through drifted snow.
My cheeks are scratched by Grandpa's whiskers
and Grandma's starched apron

as they give me hugs.

I long for a wedge of mincemeat pie.

SMALLEST DAUGHTER

Her task was setting table;
three large plates on each side,
two on one end,
three small ones at the other.

Mismatched chairs sat all around
except a bench at that end
for the three little kids.
She longed for a big plate
and a chair of her own.

ARTIST RELAXING

Cumulus clouds, May's and June's
lazy in an azure sky,
take me once more
to a cellar door.

Little girl, pinafore
tucked around knees,
her hair Dutch-boy style,
relaxed, without guile

imagined a place, an isle;
saw it in the sky-ocean.
Shut eyes tight, facing sun,
untensed lids until one

color, not to be outdone,
chased another through her head;
fireworks commanded at will

colored her isle with greenish hill,

edged the trees with orange frill
lighted her place with reddish glow.
Swirling bluebirds would not stay--
ethereal as if Monet

had come with brush to join her play.
The cellar door sloped to the south
so she might lie there afternoons
arranging clouds, coloring moons.

AFTER-SCHOOL CHORE

Just tall enough to reach the ironing board,
I toted flat irons from the kitchen range
to living room beside the radio
to smooth out pillowcases, handkerchiefs,
dishtowels, aprons, sometimes denim shirts...
the only laundry Mother deemed to trust
to my severely basic expertise.

By accident or sometimes true intent
I did not iron those pesky apron strings
but hung them in the pantry on their hook,
then Mother brought them back and frowned at me.
I never wear nor iron an apron now
though when I touch up "cotton, ten per cent"
somehow, my mother stands there by my side.

BALANCING ACT

The lion,
actually two girls
in four-legged costume,
prances nimbly atop
huge rubber ball

circling center ring
of Ringling Brothers,
Barnum & Bailey Circus.

In mind's eye
it is I, at seven,
traveling length
of farm yard
perched precariously,
arms flailing for balance,
barefoot on a barrel.

HOME BEAUTIFICATION

Single stems erupt
through cracks in sidewalk,
project in every direction.
Flesh-colored tentacles
covered with oval leaves,
produce lush, green mats.

As children, we lay on stomachs,
dug below soil
to snap off taproots,
carried our trophies home
to become Aubusson rugs
for our dirt-floor playhouse.

COUNTRY KIDS AT CHRISTMAS IN THE THIRTIES

We pestered parents, kin, neighbors
to purchase Christmas Seals,
for there were prizes for those who sold most.

We learned our lines;
    O Little Town
    Up On The Housetop

Jesus Loves Me
Merry Christmas, everyone!
performed on makeshift stages
curtained with donated sheets.

We found where Mother hid
dark-brown fruitcake,
snitched samples.

We walked home from school, half frozen,
sat on parlor heater,
wet clothes steaming, reeking.
Siblings learned not to, when one
put tongue on mailbox.

We held conferences
serious as board meetings,
decided what gifts to buy
with quarters from Dad
clutched in mittened hands.

We tied on ill-fitting skates,
headed for rippled ice
that covered low spot in pasture.

We carried corncobs and set table
with unusual diligence
for Santa Claus was coming to town.

CHRISTMAS, 1936

With three dollars in their mittens,
three little kids
searched Kresge and Woolworth
for gifts for six older siblings
and their parents;
twenty nine cents for Dad's
chocolate covered cherries,
thirty-nine

for Mom's diamond brooch

then splurged
at forty-nine cents each
for two music boxes,
averaged thirty-two
for scarves or sox for brothers,
left two cents apiece
for treats for weary,
happy shoppers.

CIRCLES

In near-dark
groups assembled
after meetings,

all ages together;
we hadn't thought
of segregating by size.

4-H Club and Luther League
were excuses
for gathering in circles

to play Farmer In The Dell
Red Rover, Red Rover,
to spin the bottle.

Emotions ran high.
Would a certain person
choose us?

We chanted and joined hands,
followed the rules
in a more innocent time.

WHILE MOTHER AND BABE ARE IN HOSPITAL

He trusts me to dust, make beds,
sweep, brew coffee.
I scorch his Sunday shirt.

Certain I can bake a cake,
I search the cupboards,
find "devil's food" in Mother's script;
reject it for sister-in-law's.
Some detail basic to her
eludes me. The effort fails.

My twelve-year-old heart plunges
as tears rise
and I experience an ache
that longs for Mother's arms;
wish I had used her recipe.

REMEMBERED ECSTASY

My path led past a school with kids at play;
two boys involved in swinging at midday.
The one in blue held tightly to the chains,
the other swung him round and, taking pains

to see the twist was at its uttermost
he held him still, and gazed, as if to boast.
"Why does he not let go and let him spin?"
I wondered as I watched. Then with a grin

he leaped astride the other's lap and leaned
far back. His buddy, also properly blue-jeaned
and red sweat-shirted stretched his arms full length.
They spun and held the chains with all their strength.

Around and round they twirled, almost a blur
of red and blue, red, blue. Their squeals of pure
delight evoked a scene from distant past
when brother twisted me and I spun fast.

33

GOOD OLD GOLDEN RULE DAYS

My siblings (eight) and I marched up the steps
through segregated cloakrooms to the door
where learning was inside, in books, on maps,
in chalk in teachers' hands; where blackboards bore

the lesson plans and math for all eight grades;
where green construction paper was the frame
for artwork we produced; where recess was
a time for choosing sides to play a game.

We gathered the erasers after school;
with gusto pounded them on the cement.
Some teachers deemed the duty a reward
while others made it seem like punishment.

By twos we trudged across to neighbor farm
to pump into the pail that we set down
fresh water for the jar with spigot. We
thought it was just as fancy as in town.

Our practice teachers yearly came and went.
The college monitored their expertise.
We rag-tag country kids helped hone their skills
and some big boys destroyed their sense of peace.

McGuffy's Readers were not then in vogue.
We learned "See Dick. See Jane. See Spot." We pledged
allegiance to the flag each day, then sang
ten minutes from our songbooks, golden edged.

Skirt tucked beneath my bloomers, stockings off
I climbed the flagpole to the top one day
then slid back down and played hopscotch again.
The boys who dared me turned and walked away.

As little kids we learned our ABCs
and without trying, heard fifth grade recite.
In lofty eighth grade, burdened with world news
reviewed sub-consciously the fifth grade rite.

With fervor and with dread we took exams
to earn our passage from the one-room school
to town where every subject had its room
and homework was a customary rule.

Some treated us as bumpkins for a while,
but most were fine in class and some excelled.
Four years of high school tested us again;
the groundwork from that single room upheld.

RECALLING DISTRICT 21

Anticipation fills me as I plan
reunion with those kids I knew in school.
Adults, now, whom I have not seen in years;
my Christmas cards go to a very few.
The task I've set will not be done in weeks--
the finding of dispersed friends, neighbors all.

In memory, I see us as we'd all
coast downhill on a sled, and then we'd plan
the other winter games to fill the weeks
that country kids, at recess played at school.
Store bought accouterments for play were few
and not expected, those depression years.

Attending that brick schoolhouse for eight years,
we each learned we must study and we all
learned that rewards of bluffing were but few.
Each teacher had a strict recital plan
and was determined in her heart to school
us in the subjects scheduled for the weeks.

Each season had its games. In fall for weeks
baseball was played each day, heedless of years
(the small ones chosen last) on teams in school
yard where sometimes the big kids let them all
steal first to second. There was not a plan
excluding any child. There were a few

who knew the rules and played umpire. Some few
would climb the flagpole barefooted. For weeks
in spring, without forethought or any plan
we segregated, boys to roll for years'
accumulated marbles. We girls all
shared secrets, lunches, boyfriends...giggled; school

days often we were on our knees on school
walks, playing jacks or chalking out a few
marked squares for hopscotch. Then in summer all
through days of helping Mom and counting weeks
till classes start, we spent those tender years
without a thought of a reunion plan.

Now, as I plan regrouping of the school
I wonder, "Have the years been good? A few
I've seen in recent weeks. I miss them all.

WE WASHED THE SEPARATOR

Take heavy metal case from discs--
it seems there are fifty,
actually less--
remove smelly residue from its edge.
Thread discs onto wire rack.
Numbered, they must be kept
in correct rotation.

Rinse before immersing
in meager lye soapsuds.
Wash each disc separately,
as well as spouts and strainer.
Rinse again with boiling water,
shake discs,
turn all upside down in dishpan.

Our least favorite task,
we bargained other chores
to avoid performing it.

SORTING MOTHER'S THINGS

The photos that we found are black and white
of kin we recognize, and some we don't--
a gentleman with goatee on his chin
and uncle with his pack of cigarettes;
a neighbor with the plaque that honored him,
Aunt Sophie's diamond pin upon her breast.
Our Grandpa and his twin are quite alike
No one can name the gentleman in back.

Hair frames a face in classic Dutch-boy cut
in shot portraying skinny little girl.
A bow accents a collar of white lace
on polka-dotted dress with set-in sleeves.
her aunt, photographer, placed her on seat
of velvet and wrought iron. The tot is I.

THE FAIR REMAINS THE SAME

In fifty years, we find there is not much
that has not changed. Today you cannot touch
the prices we paid then. And skirts have been
from ankle up to thigh, down, up again.

Now VCRs, computers and TVs
are common-place in homes, and all of these
were unheard of when I was just a kid.
To entertain ourselves, here's what we did:

We planted rows of vegetables or flowers
then watered, weeded on our knees for hours.
We sewed a dress or baked a pie or cake
or raised a pig or chicken we might take

at end of summer to the County Fair.
There was not more excitement anywhere.
The barns were full of horses, cows and sheep
and boys threw blankets on the straw to sleep.

The carnival set up its own midway
and lured us to their stands that we might play
the games of chance, though seldom did we win
the larger prizes. But we still went in.

Our moms displayed their pickles packed with dill
and dads went over to machinery hill.
Our grandma's quilts quite often won a prize
and uncle's spuds and cukes were just right size.

If one were just a little tyke he'd ride
the carousel with mother by his side;
the next year drive a car or train or boat
and wave his hand as he went by, and gloat.

The older youth held tightly in their hands
the coins for candy apples at the stands
and rides on Tilt-A-Whirl or Ferris Wheel
and chance to win a watch or squiggly eel.

Woodworking projects shone with hand-rubbed glow
and dresses sewn with care hung in a row.
By demonstrating skills that they had learned
red, blue and purple ribbons could be earned.

Some projects now may be computerized;
rewards for excellence are realized
in much the same way they were years ago
when folks brought out the best they had to show.

Of all the pleasures we enjoy today
the County Fair can still show us the way
to have good times just like they used to be...
I think I hear an old calliope!

EDNA'S HOSPITALITY

As surely as spring brings lilacs,
Saturday brought chocolate cake
to that wood-range kitchen--
recipe-book cake with thick frosting--
and bananas sliced into red jello.

Earlier, egg money in hand
on weekly trip to town,
she bought groceries, splurged
at Central Cafe on coffee and donut,
came home, scrubbed floors,
baked pies for Sunday.

Next morning, meatloaf and potatoes baking,
she warmed her Methodist soul at church.
Dinner for family followed,
but not the cake and jello.
Those she reserved for "lunch"
along with hearty sandwich makings
against the possibility of visitors.

Of course, they came,
and went away fulfilled--
not only at table.

AUNTS ETHEL

Mother's sister, Ethel, was a photographer
who printed my picture on a postcard.
I learned to ride a bicycle
the summer spent with her.

Father's sister, Ethel, never married
but had spools and marbles
and card games for us to play,
and treasures untold came to light
when we sorted her belongings after she left us.

"Aunt Ethel Number Three" was no kin at all
but appreciated the title.
When I worked for bed and board as a teen
she nurtured me.

STERLING AUNTS

As pudgy fingers,
wielding knife too large,
pare thick, short
peelings from potatoes,
the maiden aunts arrive,
offer to help,
lay aside
chic hats and handbags.

the child watches,
wide-eyed,
as long, thin, narrow curls
fall from beneath
their knives.
They place elliptical tubers
in the kettle
beside her spuds,
all planes and angles.

The girl and her siblings
suppose they are quite rich,
judging by their attire,
or quite poor,
considering
the vegetables they cultivate,
the cellar full of canned goods
they preserve each fall,
the fact they make rag rugs
to sell and take in clothing
for alterations, among
other frugalities.
Some forty year later

the girl purchases solid silver
with the aunts' legacy.

OUR OWN UNCLE SAM

His name was Earl
but Dad called him Sam.
He'd show up unannounced
and charm us kids.
We thought it strange
someone old as Dad
was not married.

He called Mother Lony
and she pretended to hate it--
her name was Leona.
He and Dad played cribbage
before chores, after dinner,
after chores.
He never helped with chores--
Mom thought he ought to.
I think he worked for the railroad.

He came at Christmas once,
attended our country school program.
Though Glen forgot most of his piece,
Sam convinced him he'd been great.

He would go to town for tobacco
in his shiny car
and take us little kids along,
buy us candy.
We watched, fascinated,
as he rolled cigarettes,
licked the paper, smoothed it down.

He'd stay a few days,
leave a hole in our lives
when he left.

GRANDMA'S APRON

Cotton, ample, rick-rack edged,
it covered her front
and sometimes sides and back,
ostensibly to keep dresses clean.
Starched and pressed,
it served many purposes.

Held by bottom corners,
it became a basket
for carrying eggs, chicken feed,
vegetables.

Flapped from the waist,
it shooed puppies from flower beds
and chicks into coops when it rained.
Children hid behind it,
wiped tears on it.
Always handy, aprons converted
to potholders, hand towels.

When telling guests goodbye outside,
Grandma rolled the apron
up around her arms
to form a sweater.

Its afterlife, with strings cut off,
was lived as a dust cloth.

GRANDMOTHER'S GIFTS

I sprinkle salt and pepper
from six-sided glass jars
with silver lids,
am transported to Grandma's,
the condiments in her hands.

She has risen early

to prepare cream of wheat
for visiting family.
I wake in privileged spot,
a cot in kitchen corner
where I may watch
this fascinating lady with magic hands;

hands that stitched needlepoint
now displayed in dozens of homes,
that pushed stick-pins
into a map on the wall
at all the places she and Grandpa visited,
that did water color
after eyesight no longer allowed needlework;
hands that learned to type letters
with carbon so each family received weekly.

When she and Grandpa moved to town
she gave me the salt and peppers
and a place setting of red-handled flatware
I had admired.

Before entering Elder Home
she distributed treasures among family.
With my surviving parent gone,
we sort and divide cherished pieces
of sentiment from two generations.

I see the cellar door
in that farmhouse kitchen
that I only passed through
if holding her hand.
I have made another passage
since Dad died,
have hands of spouse and children
to hold through their scary places,
and the knowledge that
the sturdy past is a part of me.

THREE GENERATIONS OF FOOTWORK

Thirteen year old granddaughter
plays tennis at the school's
court. As I watch her matches,
full innocent of rules,
I hear such words as match point,
and love and fault and rally
and deuce and set, advantage.
I've trouble keeping tally.

Long coltish legs tanned tawny
beneath white cotton shorts
that peek below a tee shirt
dance nimbly on the courts.
Not long ago her mother
pranced Main Street on parade,
baton twirled through her fingers
when she was in third grade.

I went to one-room schoolhouse
some fifty years ago.
Not much of what we did there
was done for public show.
We played hopscotch at recess
on every balmy day.
We skipped through squares on sidewalk
and skirts got in the way.

40th CLASS REUNION

The faces in the squares in orderly
sequence (our queen, the oaf, the brain, athlete)
evoke more sure response than formerly
since, after forty years, we choose to meet.

Our queen, still lovely, has a touch of gray;
the oaf, a booming business in the state;
the brain, one time a doctor, chose to stay

down on the farm, and till it with his mate.

We mingle, clasp each other's hands, embrace.
The nametags aid our recognition when
a voice, familiar to us calls; we face
a body not at all like it was then.

We find old cliques and class forever gone
and only fondest memories linger on.

50th CLASS REUNION

White-haired football captain
reads thirty-nine names.
His wife, our queen,
arranges carnations
for each;
red or white--
school colors.

In silence, we watch,
survivors
from class of '47
as images of carefree days
and remembered faces
enter consciousness.

REMEMBERING MY FARM

It was not my farm, of course,
nor even Father's.
Those depression days
he rented from a life insurance firm.

That farm is mine only in memory;
small, white frame house
with screened-in porch

where Topsy crawled under
to whelp her puppies.
We posed for family pictures
by our seldom-used front entry,
hollyhocks for background.
Slant of cellar door on sunny side
encouraged book reading, day dreaming.

Haymow of red barn held scent
of its contents. Kids and cousins romped in it
and one fell down the trapdoor.
Roof's pitch on granary was slight;
an adventure, there, to walk or hide or run.

Old stump that five children holding hands
could not embrace was never removed,
became site of games and tom-foolery.
Tin can thrown to sky by lit firecrackers
plummeted, cut gash on brother's head.
Mother's nasturtiums, zinnias and asters
flourished beside the stump
if her little fence
kept chickens and puppies out.

We trudged the long driveway
to pick up mail--or turn right
and visit neighbors whose children
joined us at club meetings by "Halfway Bush."
Mother planted vegetables
we must weed, then help preserve.
It was bane of girls' existence;
boys' adversary, cockleburs, they attacked
with hoes between rows of corn.

I went back once.
Granary was gone,
house and barn replaced by new,
driveway seemed much shorter.

HOUSE NOT BUILT FOR ELEVEN

I see a white frame house,
almost too small, surrounded
by tall trees and lilac bushes,
enter and smell
kitchen table's new oilcloth.
Mother presides at cupboard,
flour from tip-out bin on her apron.
Sister brings plates from pantry
while another grudgingly washes
chimneys of kerosene lamps.

I see myself tote pan of potatoes to peel
from dirt-floor cellar
lined with canned fruits and vegetables.

Brother brings enamel pail of water
from windmill for drinking,
replaces dipper.
Sibling pours bucket of cistern water
into reservoir of wood range,
removes five gallon pail
of waste below sink.
Big boys are helping dad milk cows.

I see us later, near battery-powered radio
listening to Fibber McGee and Molly.

I feel heat from parlor stove chimney
that extends through boys' room
where they sleep in two beds, three in each,
after trudging through pantry,
up stairs and through girls' room
where we three share a bed.

Walls of both rooms are covered
with calcimine that peels off
into constantly changing shapes
that nine children spend waking hours
imagining to be birds or planes or camels.

Parents' bed is covered
with hand-made star quilt.
In bottom drawer of chiffonier
is long braid I twined about my head,
that once was Mother's hair.

I am surrounded at Family Reunion;
closeness in that house
remains a part of who each of us is today.

RELUCTANT POULTRY

There was poetry in poultry
with minds of their own.

They arrived in pasteboard flats divided
into quarters with air holes poked out;
yellow puffballs that peeped and huddled into corners
of excelsior-floored boxes.

Lifted from bondage at brooder house
they hopped from our hands,
scooted under circular stove hood.
Instinct brought them to feeders
and glass-domed waterers
brothers and I kept filled.

Chores were light through sunny days
as fluff gave way to feathers.
At sudden showers Mother urged us out
to shoo chicks inside and they resisted,
bunched up in yard-fence corners.

After a month they tasted freedom
from enclosure, gleaned farmyard at large,
sometimes trespassed open granary doors.

In autumn came the challenge.
Roosted on high branches,

they eluded us as we climbed trees
to snare and carry them down;
to sort roosters into crates for selling,
from pullets housed
to provide winter breakfast.

Mother nonchalantly reached beneath hens
recovering eggs,
but I carried a stick and held their heads
against side of the nest before groping under them.
And they pecked me.

I did not think them poetic then.

AT LENTEN SERVICE

Elderly visiting pastor
chooses that we sing
"What A Friend We Have In Jesus."
Small matter I cannot see the words
for moisture in my eyes.
Verses are engraved in my childhood
along with "I pledge allegiance."

Like a procession before me
pass ample ladies
(more used to print dresses and aprons)
in Sunday best, though it is Wednesday.

Not only my eyes remember,
but I smell egg coffee,
thick brown bread sandwiches,
rosettes and kringla.
Good cooks all,
those Swedish Lutheran ladies
who welcomed my mother,
non-Scandinavian Methodist,
into their monthly Ladies' Aid.
She, one-time piano teacher,

accompanied their singing.

I see the hand-hewn wooden box,
very like a coffin,
their men transported
from house to house across the prairie
with thick china plates and cups,
flatware, Bibles and songbooks inside.
I see blonde, blue-eyed children,
with whom I played, attended Luther League,
learned their catechism.

Even overalled husbands of the ladies
pass by to threshing machine
while we sing all four verses
of "What A Friend We Have In Jesus."

LEST WE FORGET

First were previews
then, news;
black and white jeeps, tanks, soldiers,
American flags, fighter planes,
dogfights in the sky--B-29s spiraling down.
Roosevelt and Churchill met.
Stiff-legged marchers
saluted the mustached Fuhrer.

Next, Loony Tunes--
mice, cats, rabbits, birds
chased, evaded, fell down holes,
went berserk to make us laugh.
MGM lion roared.
Lauren Bacall tossed hair from her eyes,
Doris Day played 40s women,
Bob, Bing and Dorothy went on the road.
"Thirty Seconds Over Tokyo,"
"Bridge On The River Kwai,"
"Mrs. Miniver," kept the horror before us.

Today they march to front of auditorium--
Legionnaires and Veterans of Foreign Wars--
carry the colors, the guns
to Hup, Hu, Hree, Hor of former sergeant.
Mayor reads the orders,
student recites Gettysburg address,
boy and girl scouts place wreaths,
school band plays "The Star Spangled Banner."
We stand as one
before a gun salute, taps.

Reels in our heads roll--
jeeps, tanks, soldiers, stars and stripes
account for the mist in our eyes.

BRAVE OLD MAN

Hot coffee, thick sandwiches,
chocolate cake had been served
mid-morning to men.

Five years old that summer,
I tagged after Mother,
was allowed to stay;
watched from car
near the rig.

Horses reared, charged
from beside thresher.
Wagon tongue
split Ford's back window.
Old gentleman
who measured grain
had seen them coming,
snatched me away.

He walked across town
to church
the day I married.

NOVEMBER 11, THE BIG ONE

Each winter stories surface,
with ever less who remember.

Without warning a strange sky
with high winds dropped a blizzard
that swirled to second stories,
became hard and crusty.
Horses pulled sleighs over mounds
where phone lines barely showed.

Farmers tethered to doorknobs
searched for barns found by instinct only,
followed ropes back to kitchen warmth.

Fathers performed chores of children
not allowed out,
brought in coal and corncobs for fire,
water for drinking and washing.

Mothers trimmed wicks,
hoarded kerosene for lamps
used night and day.

Children stomped cream in a jar,
watched for specks of butter,
for there was no way
to get to school.

After the storm, sunshine
urged little people out to dig caves,
follow mazes of paths
scooped to outbuildings,
think it all an adventure;
now tell the story
to grandchildren.

20TH CENTURY COMMUNICATION

I remember penny postcards.
Aunts' messages arrived
inviting us for Sunday dinner,
or, those days, they invited themselves
to our place.

Mother's small script
went up-hill.
She filled that bottom corner,
then up the left side,
over the top and back down
the margin.

Dad's family, farther flung,
had a Circle Letter he sent
to Aunt Mary who shared it
with Grandpa and Grandma
and maiden Aunts living with them;
then on to the Uncles in Iowa,
to return to us
from Aunt Anna in Pennsylvania.

During the war we wrote on
thin paper and envelopes
with red and blue edges
for letters to brothers overseas.

Telephone was used
for local calls only.

The Round Robin my brother started
has circulated among my siblings
over forty years.

Our children use E-Mail.

AWASH IN CIRCLES OF MEMORY

I pick them from their places--
ewers, bowls, vases of china and crystal,
sponge them in warm suds,
rinse and wipe.

The pitcher with 24 carat gold finish,
mailed from California to midwest
for my parents' fiftieth anniversary
is returned to honored place.

Pieces bought after touring crystal factories
in Norway and Ireland are given new glow.
Many were gifts;
those purchased at auctions of friends,
neighbors and kin were "everyday" to them,
precious to me.

Faces appear as I handle each one:
Aunt Ethel, never married,
Lula, famous at potlucks and Circle lunches,
Mrs. Putnam, mayor's wife, purchaser
of my sponge cakes at bake sales,
Mother-in-law, wearer of aprons and smiles,
Winston, former boss, provider
of this pitcher as centerpiece
at my retirement party,
Verna, his mother, from whose things
I was honored to choose,
Donald, his CPA cousin,
visitor at our office,
Callie whose daughter gave me back
a piece that had been from Mom,
Elfie, whom we visited in Germany,
Velva, lady I "adopted" in Nursing Home,
Lucille dear friend going blind,
Bill, for whom I answered telephone
for three decades,
LaDonna, Deb and Sue, daughters
who have added to the collection,

and Dad, who came from Pennsylvania
a hundred years ago
with Grandma and the big blue pitcher.

I notice circles left when I raise them--
pressed into doilies,
or even on dust in high places.
The circles bear a story;
treasures brought into the 1900s,
used for generations,
will be left to LaDonna, Deb and Sue
to be treasured in another century.

YOU CAN'T HAVE IT BOTH WAYS

Eight-sided red signs held up traffic
with help from a cop on Saturday nights
when the movie let out in my home town.
One store's revolving door made a small girl
skip smartly that it might not snap her heels.

I faced four cars abreast
yesterday, going wrong way
on one-way street
that was not so designated
when I was a girl.

Roof over Front Street
effects a mall; there's an escalator
where we once drove.
They've demolished the bridge
by the station where we waited for trains
carrying junk iron and old tires
for the war effort.
Vehicles cross the river on a curved
concrete span, oblivious of trains below.

Popcorn wagon's space is converted
to a traffic lane, sending autos

to parking places stacked up.
Semaphores have buttons with instructions;
PRESS FOR WALK SIGNAL.

I put a casserole in the microwave
as I mourn the home town
no longer there.

SUBLIME SWINE

Pink baby pigs
sprawled in a pile
on straw Dad provided,
squirmed and squealed.
As patient sow laid down,
piglets untangled themselves,
lined up like buttons on an abacus
to suckle.

I stood tip-toed on bottom plank
that I might see over
top board of pen,
watch that mothering.

Little pink pigs
sprawl in a pile in a box.
Little girl squirms and squeals
as Mother buys for her
a Beanie Baby.

LITTLE GIRLS AND ROSES

Along the fences, in the wood and field
wild roses flourish, scenting summer air.
In scraggly clumps they bloom and bunches yield
a garland little girls twine in their hair.

These girls, when wed, will choose a white tea rose
to fill their bridal baskets and bouquets
and hold them proudly at their breasts and pose
for photos they will treasure all their days.

As matrons they will garden on their knees
and plant the noble hybrids; Arctic Flame
and Helen Hayes and Lily Pons and Peace
and every hardy, thornless one can name

while memory pictures field and wood and fence
and childish aprons filled with fragrant scents.

INTO THE PAST

Dad, Mother, Merle, Lorene, long gone,
smile from the video--grandparents, too.

Daughter garnered pictures
from each of my siblings,
arranged them in orderly fashion--
oldest to youngest,
though she reversed Lyle and Maurice.

Harold in World War II uniform
Merle smiling by RV
Lorene surrounded by family
Inez (two or three years old)
   holding barred-rock hen
three daughters and I
   in matching dresses
Glen and Wayne in Boy Scout finery
spouses in wedding and family pictures
children and grandchildren
   in school snaps

Mother with her brothers and sisters
   at family reunion
slender, black-haired Dad

pulling little Harold (now nearly eighty)
in wagon in old photo
with those ragged white edges

Music in the background--
mostly Mother playing piano--
tunes Lyle recorded years past;
tunes part of our childhood,
part of who she was.

Nearly a decade ago
we gathered for Mom's 90th birthday
and saw the video for the first time.
She left us soon after.

Watching now, I understand
her tender smile
as tears slid down her cheeks.

A LOVELY PATH

I remember a path.
When I am sad
it was a happy path.
When I am poor
it was a lucrative path.
When I am cold
it was a warm path.
When I am lonely
it was a friendly path.
When I am hurting
it was a comfortable path.
When I am angry
it was a peaceful path.

I never really walked that path.
It is the "what if" path
we imagine
to get us through the hard places.

Had I taken that other path
would I have known
the joys, the memories
I treasure now?

PAST AND FUTURE UTOPIAS

Animal scents and sounds,
sunsets and thunderstorms,
barbed wire fences and clotheslines,
kerosene lamps and lanterns,
windmills and cisterns,
lettuce and zinnias,
baby chicks and setting hens,
horse-drawn plows and haystacks,
homemade bread and pancakes,
chambray shirts and bib overalls,

the smell of cottage cheese
or baked beans simmering,
crisp sheets
perfumed by the whole outdoors,
and the annual invasion
of threshing crews
comprised rural life.

Our names will be engraved
at scattered places one day,
but our spirits will hark back there
and linger awhile before going on
to that other paradise.